Undone

Haley Nicole Boone

Copyright © 2019 Haley Nicole Boone

All rights reserved.

ISBN-13: 9780692187814

DEAR READER

I pray this book of words you hold in your hand will one day transform into a pencil, an instrument, or a paintbrush for you to share your own story. Your story isn't over yet; your life is simply undone. One day, I hope you see yourself the way Jesus sees you, for you are so loved.
Thank you for reading.

CONTENTS

1	Seeing Blue	1
2	To My Own Two Hands	14
3	One Way Conversations in Red	25
4	Yellow	36
	About the Author	50

ACKNOWLEDGMENTS

My deepest thanks to the lovely people who have not only supported my writing, but have shaped me into the person I am today. Thank you, to every teacher who taught me how to write, my parents who encouraged me to write, Anxiety that gave me a reason to write, and God who gave me a passion to write. Thank you, Mrs. Anna Harris-Parker, for mentoring me through this entire publishing process. You are such a lovely, inspiring woman. God bless you.

SEEING BLUE

Haley Nicole Boone

My eyes are the bluest of blues when I'm crying.
When the tears are pouring out of my eyes,
slipping down my checks.
When there's harsh redness
where there once was white.
When you can see the pain in my eyes.
How tragic it is that my favorite color is blue.

Undone

I'm a broken heart.
I'm half reality, half fantasy.
I'm constantly being pulled between what is real and what I've made up.
Which side do I choose?
Which path do I take?
One half of my heart is asleep.
How can I wake it to be combined with reality?
How can I make these opposite halves a complete and equal whole?
Wake up! Wake up!
You're feeding the awake half sleeping pills.
I don't want to be blinded by sleep.
Wake up! wake up!
Make my whole heart, beat.

You are a parasite.
You feed on the living.
You want my body as your home,
but it wasn't made for two,
it wasn't made for you.
You are toxic.
You make me sick.
You'll feed on my blood until my death,
infesting me with your poisonous flow,
but I have plans that don't involve you.
I have dreams that you can never share.
You can't control me.
It's over.
I'm done.
But, you left the smell of death on my soul.
It's become my own stench
that only I can recognize.
It dwells around me,
hovering over my body,
but I'll keep fighting the odor,
using bug spray as perfume
because you are a pest
and somehow I've become your host,
but I didn't invite you.

Undone

I constantly feel like someone is chasing me yet there is,
but that someone is not a someone,
it's a something
and that something has a name--
Anxiety.
It follows me like a shadow.
It holds me down until I am
drowning in tears,
screaming for help.
Yet my screams are silent.
There's no splashes in my waves of tears
for anyone to hear or notice me.
I'm trying so hard to swim to the top,
but I'm sinking so fast to the bottom,
I've already given up.

I walk behind slow people
while fast people walk behind me.
I'm trying my best to pick up my speed,
but the people in front of me are slowing me down.
I can't seem to get around them
and soon I'm trampled by the crowd behind me.

Undone

There is a monster that lives in me.
It calls me friend,
partner,
but I call it enemy.

There's a bag full of Anxiety covering my head,
tied around my neck.
I'm choking,
suffocating,
begging to be free
But this bag that holds me hostage
keeps my voice caged in
next to a hungry lion
who feeds on the fear of words.

Undone

Trapped in.
Trapped out.
Trapped between.
You've seen my need.
Crying and bleeding.
Just pleading to be free.
Can't you see?
You have my mind locked on this routine.
I need you to see what's underneath.
I've been gritting my teeth.
My hair is falling out every week.
What is the purpose for me to seek?
I can't see above the deep water holding me
down,
down,
drown!
I can't fight the currents.
I'm still sinking,
but I've already hit the ground.
Trapped in.
Trapped out.
Trapped between.
This isn't for me.

I don't think you understand--
everything I do has to have a plan, maybe three.
I'm running faster than the stop lights turn to green
My heart is beating 1, 2, 3
I shut the door without a peek
This is the only time I ever get some peace
I feel like someone is chasing me
I have spiders crawling from my head down to my feet
I can't outrun this shadow attached to my own feet
I'm running faster than the stop lights turn to green
I can't breathe!
Oh, I can't breathe!
You make me feel like, make me feel like
a broken record on repeat
Oh, I can't breathe.

Undone

You didn't break down my wall,
You built it.
You made the clay bricks yourself
and placed them around me,
forming the cage my mind now lives in.
You didn't set the real me free.
You locked me up and decided you had authority over
the key.

Haley Nicole Boone

I wish you understood the monster inside of me.
If he lived in you, I promise I'd give you empathy.
But you give no sympathy
for the monster that lives in me.
And all I do is not speak
because people give me Anxiety,
which builds the monster inside of me.

Undone

Trying to live fearless in the name of Jesus--
shaking in my seat,
gasping every beat.
I can't take another defeat.
This fear is killing me.
I have hope for the future to come,
but Anxiety whispers, "what if you're wrong?"
I'm sinking,
I'm swimming,
then everything repeats.
What if this fear will be the death of me?
What if I can't overcome the unseen,
the unknown,
the unimaginable?
What if my mind tick tocks until it stops?
What if I can't be fearless?
Lord, make me be
because I'm my own enemy
and this friend I call Anxiety
is eating at me
and I know I'll soon be eaten alive in misery
A feast for the worry that lives in me.

TO MY OWN TWO HANDS

Undone

Leaving my body to heal itself
from the damage I have done
All I'm left with are the scars
I have given myself
all by myself
from myself
to bring pain to myself
as I try to fix myself

Private eyes
I'll keep them disguised.
Burning
Red
Flashing
Drip
Filtered through
Salt caught in the creases
Keep them in
Filter through
You watch me,
as I watch myself, too.
Messy blue--
what are you calling me to?
Filter through
Watching myself through blue,
as You watch me through a new hue
Private eyes hidden from the light
Colorful runs
under my palms
Wiped
Smeared
You watch my private eyes
disguised by the light
Hurting
Twisting
Nearly going dry
Raw
Squinting through it all
Filtered through
I'm changing, too.

Undone

I wrote you an escape plan to leave my body,
but the exit was blocked
and somehow my body was fighting against me,
telling you to stay

Maybe it's okay to sit in a room
where the temperature is a notch too high than you prefer
just to feel the sweat trickle down your hairline
just to hear your panting breath
to finally realize that you are breathing
right here
right now
alive…
Maybe it's okay to scream your heart out
until your throat is sore
and your voice is faint
just to know you have a voice
a story to tell
a mouth that works
Maybe it's okay to find yourself crying
just to feel the tears
to taste the saltiness
to be still
just to know that at least your body is doing one thing right today-
producing tears.
Maybe, just maybe, it's okay
to take multiple long showers in one day
just to feel the water wash the soap down your back
just to feel clean
just to feel that you have a body
just to feel human
Or maybe these are the things I tell myself
just to feel a slight bit normal
as my numbness fades and my senses start working again.

Undone

You're just a dark silhouette of me
Lacking personality
Not even half of the whole in me
When the light turns on
everyone can see
the glimpse of you is not reality

Haley Nicole Boone

When you are trying to discover who you are,
don't go to the mirror,
go to your art.

And yet all those rabbit holes I fell through didn't lead me to *Wonderland*,
they lead me to *Neverland*--
a home for the lost souls who dwell on their purpose.
It's a suicide trap--
waiting for someone to find you in this place.
You can never escape.
I ran out of pixie dust
and a whole lot of faith.

Haley Nicole Boone

Anxiety is a full grown person who lives inside of me.
He used to be bigger than me
heavier,
taller,
older,
but as I'm learning to control him
he shrinks,
he loses weight.
I've learned his tricks,
his schemes.
I've learned when he wakes up and when he falls asleep.
I know his whole routine.
So, one day when he's the size of my thumb
I'll cough him out
like a virus,
all gone.

Undone

I hear screaming.
I look out the window to see nothing but greenery.
I thought it was the neighbors' children playing in the streets.
I turn away and hear the loud screams begin to cry out again.
I race to the window once more.
I see nothing.
Passing by a mirror,
I see the screams coming out of my chest.
It is me who screams.
It is my insides screaming out so loud.
I want to be heard; I want to be listened to,
but how can you hear me if I can't even recognize my own screams?
I'm drifting as I feel my heart slowing down with every beat.
Beep...beep...beep.
I'm gone.
But you didn't even hear a peep.

I can't tell you who's my friend
or my enemy.
I'm still trying to figure out if I'm my own friend
or enemy.

ONE WAY CONVERSATIONS IN RED

Haley Nicole Boone

You're actually one of the wildflowers
growing by the stream--
planted by the water,
thriving in between.
You make things happy--
your growing, yellow hue,
but you can't see yellow yet
and it's killing you
because all you see is blue.

Undone

No more waging wars.
The battle you keep fighting alone in your head--
Stop!
Drop your weapon.
God has already won the battle.
Why do you keep stabbing dead bodies?
The war is over.
It's finished!

Haley Nicole Boone

You're a deep one, my darling,
but they don't think of you the same.
They see you as crazy or even insane.
The birds fly high above you,
but they are higher than the birds.
Take this pen and ground them
only with your words.

Undone

You thought that was your ceiling?
That was only the floor,
your waking ground of growth--
onto the next door.
God has so much more in store:
stairs,
elevators,
escalators,
galore.
So flip your perspective.
It's not the ceiling your head is touching;
you're just doing a headstand.
Look at the floor
and look up at the stairs--
the levels,
the journey to come.
Beyond the floor there is more in store,
so don't ignore the next door.

Haley Nicole Boone

Even if you have thrown my words away
or crumbled them in the bin;
bind the pieces back together,
take your time to find the lighter
that sparked your fire once.
Fight for Me as I fought for you.

Undone

Your mind is full of beautiful things
the world has never seen.
Paint it,
write it,
wake it,
create.
Your life was not meant to be a waste.
You have a voice to lift Me up.
You have a life that was made from dust.
Catch a leaf,
fly a kite,
make the little things bright.
You have a purpose in being here.
You have a journey beyond the sphere.
Take pictures and write.
I didn't give you life to dull your lovely light.

Fight him,
Fight them
With art,
With a pen.
Even with a limp
in your limb,
you can fight them off.
They will never win.

Undone

Open your mouth, darling;
the world is ready to hear your voice.

Be careful little one, for your own two hands
are capable of great destruction.
You can raw your wrists with the same hand that holds
the sharp edge.
Your own lips can produce the words that haunt you
the most,
spreading lies for your mind to memorize.
When you look in the mirror at night,
don't be your own enemy.

Undone

You are one of the wildflowers, my dear--
delicate in complexion,
tender to the touch.
I know you are frustrated, my dear,
but precious one, don't give up.
Just as the heavy heaps of water
would crush a dainty dandelion
in one downfall,
so would you, too, be destroyed
by all the wisdom I hold.
Take time in the pages
that may be ripped.
Seek me diligently in the red letters,
where my whispers are still crying out.
My child, continue on.
Don't turn to the world.
It will stomp you with no remorse in its heart.
The evidence is in the faith.
Keep the race.
Keep the race.
You aren't finished yet.
This story has just begun.
Your life is simply undone.

Haley Nicole Boone

YELLOW

Undone

Balancing books on my head,
I'm not a princess in training.
I don't need these unnecessary weights.
With these burdens I hold,
I can't keep my head up.
These books are holding me down.
I know more about the details on the ground.
I don't know what above looks like--
the color of the sky
or how many clouds abide.
The only glimpses I see
are the shadows of birds flying above me--
free as they should be,
free as I want to be.
But You lift my chin up,
the books fall off of my head,
tumbling down
one by one
until the weight is gone.
Down at Your feet
the burdens lie dead.
Free!
My eyes now see the yellow sunrise
through the many clouds again.

Haley Nicole Boone

Somehow, You are attracted to my brokenness
though I am a mess
and I can't even look at myself.
I am loved by You.
Your love is endless.

Undone

I'm under,
under it all--
dirt,
waste,
fertilizer--
raw.
I will have a breakthrough soon
coming through the surface
as a dandelion would.
Under it all is dark and dry,
but through it all, in You I will confide.
You are my hope in days like these.
I'm alone.
I'm hurting,
but I'm on my knees,
begging You, please,
set me free from the weight above me.

I know it's not easy to see
what this world has made of me,
but it's easy to get on track
when I know I have You patting my back,
cheering me on,
hugging me strong.
Your love never gave up on me.
Pulling me closer,
drawing me in,
You have all of my attention.
Oh, the joy I will see.
You have met all of my needs.
In You, I have and will believe
for eternity.

Undone

My eyes are getting old.
My vision is failing me in the night,
but I will try to fight.
I rub,
I blink.
There is no adjustment for me to find the light
at this pitch of night--
no spark,
no flame,
no bulb.
I can't see what's in front of me.
So, I sleep.
Inside my closed eyes, there is light--
the light that shines in the night,
the light that comes on and doesn't say goodbye.
It stays with me wherever I go.
I follow it because I know the light in the night
will guide me home.

For there is freedom
in Your hands that pull me up,
out of the pit.
I'm sick.
I'm sick of the lies,
the enemy's disguise,
this broken pain.
My mind is going insane.
I feel like serving You
Is all in vain.
What is there to gain
when there is just pain?
But Your name--
oh, Your name,
has made a way.
I will say, You reign
again and again,
forever, Amen.

Undone

Finding comfort in pages that are a little ripped,
finding comfort in words that are written in red,
holding a book that is a little bent on years,
Holding a story that is a little wet from tears.

I'm a daughter--
not just any daughter,
I'm *the* daughter.
The daughter who has many sisters and brothers reborn under the same blood.
Who is our Father? you may ask.
None other than the King of kings,
the One who sets us free,
the One who lives in me.
One day you will see
the God whom I believe,
my Father I love and He loves me.

Undone

The Bible is poetry itself
written from a foreshadow;
God allowed man to see.
The perfect alignment of words
coming together for understanding.
It's a conversation
between a Father and His children.
It's a love letter
and I'm a hopeless romantic.

Wildflowers,
honey,
and all things yummy--
Yellow is the color for me.

I am free,
I am free,
there is no reason to disagree.

In fields of green, I will be seen
by the indigos.
Vibrant in the color of the sun,
blowing in the breeze,
dancing with the trees

I am alive,
I am alive.
I won't give up.

Undone

This car is Yours, but I stole it
and left You in the passenger seat.

These dusty bones are Yours,
but I claimed them as my own.

This plane I'm flying wasn't written in my name,
but I called You my copilot.

So, take my hands,
break them off the steering wheel
mold my heart to trust You.

I don't need a cheerleader;
I need a guide whose feet never sink underwater.

Haley Nicole Boone

Here I am again
In front of You
But in yellow,
Not in blue

For I was made new
In You--
From darkness into light,
From sadness into joy.

I am alive
And now I see yellow, too.

Undone

ABOUT THE AUTHOR

Ever since I was a young child in elementary school, I have loved to write. Often times, my parents would find me sitting at the kitchen table creating stories on stapled white, printer paper. When I transitioned into middle school, I learned that I really enjoyed writing essays for my English class, which carried on into my high school years. In 10th grade, my love for poetry sparked along with a whirlwind of Anxiety. Anxiety wasn't new to me, I've battled with it for years. Instead of calling it shyness, like I once did as a child, Anxiety became known as the monster that lives in me. It became my identity and soon enough, my internal dialogue became my enemy. It whispered lies in my mind, telling me that I'm worthless and that I have no purpose being alive. I spent many moments throughout my teenage years asking God why He allowed these burdens to dictate my mind and emotions. I felt hopeless and alone.

The only thing that helped me cope with my emotions was writing poetry. My poetry allowed me to control my unwanted friend and gave me a creative voice to overpower it. After setting free all of my emotions, through writing hundreds of poems, I realized it was my passion. I dreamt of one day publishing my collection of poems in the future, so when my senior year arrived, I knew publishing my first poetry book was a great opportunity for my senior project. I spent hours deciding which poems I wanted to include, editing the poems, learning from my mentor how to better my poems, and uploading the poems to Kindle Direct Publishing. I believe this project has the potential to change a person's life in such a positive way. Although poetry is not for everyone and the struggles I write about aren't universal, someone somewhere could possibly find the hope and comfort from my words that he or she has been searching for. What's so special about my project is that it doesn't just stop; my words will continue on. My hope is that my book that readers hold in their hand will one day transform into a pencil, an instrument, or a paintbrush for others to share their own story.

Everything that I have experienced in my life thus far has prepared me for my senior project. Thank you, to every teacher who taught me how to write, my parents who encouraged me to write, Anxiety that gave me a reason to write, and God who gave me a passion to write. Someone once said, "God doesn't allow you to go through something that he's not going to use." I wholeheartedly believe this quote because I am a product of it. God used my pain and brokenness of Anxiety to not only shape me into the person He created me to be, but to create this whole book. Without going through years of suffering, this book wouldn't be in your hands today. So, thank you God for being the mastermind behind this plan, even before my existence began, and for allowing Anxiety to be a part of my life so You could use it to create something even bigger than I could ever imagine.

www.ingramcontent.com/pod-product-compliance
Lightning Source LLC
Chambersburg PA
CBHW020608030426
42337CB00013B/1269